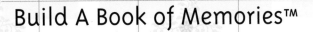

Build A Book of Memories™

My Grandchildren

A Memory Keepsake

Place a favorite photo of
you and your grandchild(ren) here.

Use Template A.

This book belongs to

_____

Build A Book of Memories™

My Grandchildren

A Memory Keepsake

© Avalanche Publishing, Inc.
ISBN 1-58622-546-4
Original text, design and concept by the
Avalanche Publishing Creative Team

Item #91006

Printed in China

01040105M

Visit our web site at
www.avalanchepub.com

Avalanche Publishing, Inc.
15262 Pipeline Lane
Huntington Beach, CA 92649
Phone (714) 898-2400 • Fax (714) 898-2410

Our Family Tree

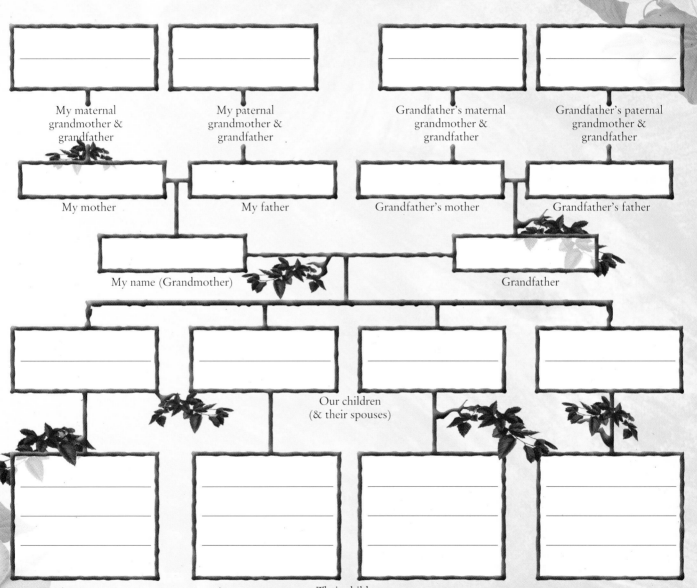

My maternal grandmother & grandfather

My paternal grandmother & grandfather

Grandfather's maternal grandmother & grandfather

Grandfather's paternal grandmother & grandfather

My mother

My father

Grandfather's mother

Grandfather's father

My name (Grandmother)

Grandfather

Our children (& their spouses)

Their children (Our Grandchildren)

My Grandbabies

"A bit of talcum
is always walcum."

—Ogden Nash

Place a grandchild's
Birth photo here.

Use Template B.

Place a grandchild's
Birth photo here.

Use Template B.

Name:

Birth Date & Time:

Length & Weight:

Parents:

Name:

Birth Date & Time:

Length & Weight:

Parents:

Name:

Birth Date & Time:

Length & Weight:

Parents:

Place a grandchild's
Birth photo here.

Use Template B.

Place a grandchild's
Birth photo here.

Use Template B.

Name:

Birth Date & Time:

Length & Weight:

Parents:

Just Hatched!

Special *Birthday* Parties

Place a grandchild's
Birthday Party photo here.

Use Template C.

Name:

Age:

Birthday Party Theme:

Memorable Party Moments:

smile for the camera!

Place a grandchild's
Birthday Party photo here.

Use Template C.

Name:

Age:

Birthday Party Theme:

Memorable Party Moments:

Memorable Party Moments: _____

_____

_____

_____

_____

Place a grandchild's
Birthday Party photo here.

Use Template C.

Name: _____

Age: _____

Birthday Party Theme: _____

Memorable Party Moments: _____

_____

_____

_____

Place a grandchild's
Birthday Party photo here.

Use Template C.

Name: _____

Age: _____

Birthday Party Theme: _____

Happy Birthday!

Place a grandchild's
Birthday Party photo here.

Use Template C.

Name:

Age:

Birthday Party Theme:

Memorable Party Moments:

_____

_____

_____

_____

_____

_____

Memorable Party Moments:

_____

_____

_____

_____

_____

_____

Place a grandchild's
Birthday Party photo here.

Use Template C.

Name:

Age:

Birthday Party Theme:

Place a grandchild's
Birthday Party photo here.

Use Template C.

Name:

Age:

Birthday Party Theme:

Memorable Party Moments:

Place a grandchild's
Birthday Party photo here.

Use Template C.

Name:

Age:

Birthday Party Theme:

Memorable Party Moments:

Kids Are So Cute...

From the first tooth to the missing tooth, from the first haircut to that stand-up cowlick—remember those memorable photo moments here!

Place a grandchild's
First Tooth photo here.

Use Template D.

Name:

Age:

Place a grandchild's
Missing Tooth photo here.

Use Template D.

Name:

Age:

Place a grandchild's
First Tooth photo here.

Use Template D.

Name:

Age:

Place a grandchild's
Missing Tooth photo here.

Use Template D.

Name:

Age:

Out of the Mouths of Babes...

Place a grandchild's
First Haircut photo here.

Use Template D.

Name:

Age:

Favorite Saying:

Record here those favorite gems
your grandchildren have said!

Place a grandchild's
Goofy Expression photo here.

Use Template D.

Name:

Age:

Favorite Saying:

Place a grandchild's
Goofy Expression photo here.

Use Template D.

Name:

Age:

Favorite Saying:

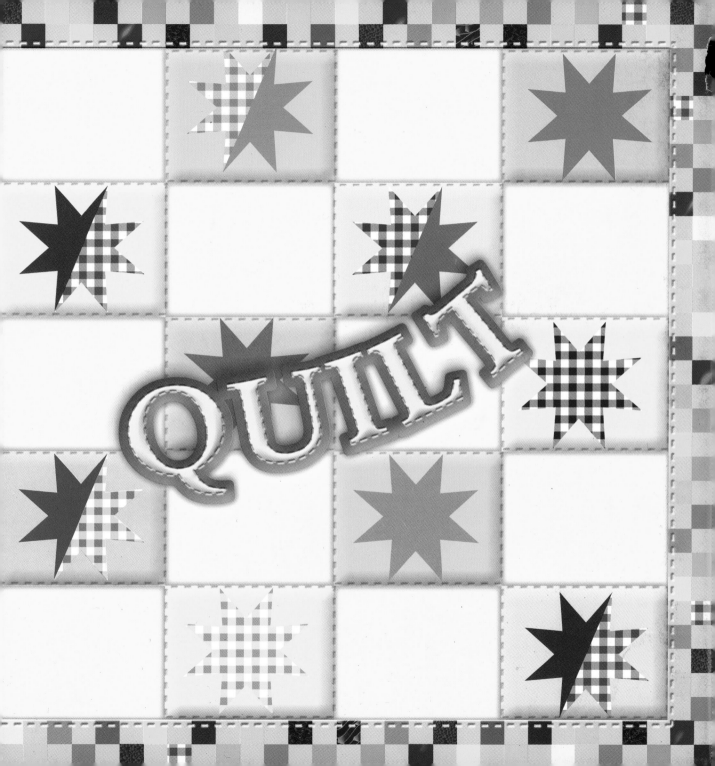

Place a *Family* photo here.

Use Template E.

Place a *Family* photo here.

Use Template E.

Place a *Family* photo here.

Use Template E.

Place a *Family* photo here.

Use Template E.

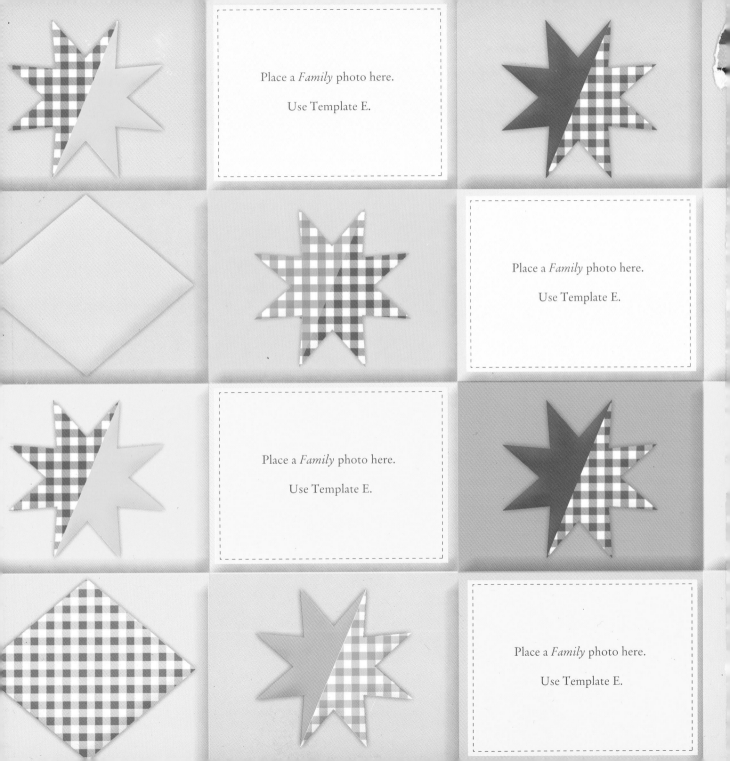

Place a *Family* photo here.

Use Template E.

Place a *Family* photo here.

Use Template E.

Place a *Family* photo here.

Use Template E.

Place a *Family* photo here.

Use Template E.

Family Cooking Treasures

My grandchildren love me to make...

Their favorite breakfast foods:
_____

_____

Their favorite lunch & dinner foods:
_____

_____

Their favorite snacks:
_____

_____

Their favorite desserts:
_____

_____

They also love to create these special foods with me:
_____

_____

_____

When I bake...

Who likes to mix the batter:
_____

_____

Who licks the spoon:
_____

_____

Who licks the bowl:
_____

_____

Who just can't wait to eat the first cookie:
_____

_____

Who shares cookies with friends and family:
_____

_____

Who cleans up:
_____

_____

My Little Helpers

Place a grandchild(ren)
In the Kitchen photo here.

Use Template F.

Holding their spatulas and spoons,
Wearing icing-wreathed smiles,
Sticky fingers and all—
Grandkids in the kitchen make everything special!

Springtime Celebrations

Place a grandchild's
Spring photo here.

Use Template G.

Place a grandchild's
Spring photo here.

Use Template G.

Name:

Age:

When:

Where:

Name:

Age:

When:

Where:

My Little Valentines

My Spring Sweethearts

Place a grandchild's *Spring* photo here.

Use Template G.

Place a grandchild's *Spring* photo here.

Use Template G.

Name: _____

Age: _____

When: _____

Where: _____

Name: _____

Age: _____

When: _____

Where: _____

Having Fun in the
Summer Sun

From their first days at camp to their first "big fish" stories,
add those treasured vacation memory photos here!

In the Swim

Place a grandchild's
Vacation photo here.

Use Template H.

At Camp

Place a grandchild's
Vacation photo here.

Use Template I.

Name:

Age:

When:

Where:

Gone Fishin'

At the Beach

Name:

Age:

When:

Where:

Vacation Time!

From their first road trips to their first plane rides, place those treasured memory photos here!

Name: _____
Age: _____
When: _____
Where: _____
_____
_____

Place a grandchild's *Vacation* photo here.

Use Template J.

Name: _____
Age: _____
When: _____
Where: _____

Place a grandchild's *Vacation* photo here.

Use Template J.

Planes, Trains, and Automobiles...

Wherever They Roam...

From local spots to foreign lands,
gather those special travel memories here!

Place a grandchild's
Vacation photo here.

Use Template K.

Place a grandchild's
Vacation photo here.

Use Template L.

Name:

Age:

When:

Where:

Name:

Age:

When:

Where:

Place a grandchild's
Vacation photo here.

Use Template M.

Place a grandchild's
Vacation photo here.

Use Template M.

Name: _____

Age: _____

When: _____

Where: _____

Name: _____

Age: _____

When: _____

Where: _____

...They'll Always

Come Home.

U.S. MAIL

The First Days
of School

nursery school

Name:

Age:

Grade:

Place a grandchild's *School* photo here.

Use Template N.

Place a grandchild's *School* photo here.

Use Template N.

kindergarten

Place a grandchild's *School* photo here.

Use Template N.

Name:

Age:

Grade:

Name:

Age:

Grade:

elementary school

Name:

Age:

Grade:

Place a grandchild's *School* photo here.

Use Template N.

grade 1

Place a grandchild's *School* photo here.

Use Template N.

grade 2

Name:

Age:

Grade:

Name:

Age:

Grade:

Place a grandchild's *School* photo here.

Use Template N.

Name:

Age:

Grade:

grade 3

Place a grandchild's *School* photo here.

Use Template N.

grade 4

Special School Days

Name:

Age:

Grade:

Place a grandchild's *School* photo here.

Use Template N.

Name:

Age:

Grade:

Place a grandchild's *School* photo here.

Use Template N.

grade 7

Name:

Age:

Grade:

Place a grandchild's
School photo here.

Use Template N.

Place a grandchild's
School photo here.

Use Template N.

Name:

Age:

Grade:

junior high

Place a grandchild's
School photo here.

Use Template N.

grade 8

Name:

Age:

Grade:

School Rules!

Place a grandchild's *School* photo here.

Use Template N.

Name:

Age:

Grade:

Place a grandchild's *School* photo here.

Use Template N.

Name:

Age:

Grade:

Place a grandchild's
School photo here.

Use Template N.

Name:

Age:

Grade:

Place a grandchild's
School photo here.

Use Template N.

diploma

Name:

Age:

Grade:

Fall Festivities

Place a grandchild's *Fall Holiday* photo here.

Use Template O.

Place a grandchild's *Fall Holiday* photo here.

Use Template P.

Name: _____

Age: _____

Holiday: _____

Costume Fun

Name: _____

Age: _____

Holiday: _____

Giving Thanks

Place a grandchild's
Fall Holiday photo here.

Use Template Q.

Name: _____

Age: _____

Holiday: _____

Place a grandchild's
Fall Holiday photo here.

Use Template R.

Name: _____

Age: _____

Holiday: _____

Winter Wonders

Happy Holidays!

Place a grandchild's
Winter Holiday photo here.

Use Template S.

Name:

Age:

Holiday:

Place a grandchild's
Winter Holiday photo here.

Use Template S.

Name:

Age:

Holiday:

Name:

Age:

Holiday:

Place a grandchild's
Winter Holiday photo here.

Use Template S.

Celebrate!

Name:

Age:

Holiday:

Place a grandchild's
Winter Holiday photo here.

Use Template S.

Our Wishing Well

Here's a place for those special hopes, dreams, and wishes.
Have your grandchild(ren) write a personal wish on a
piece of paper. Label each paper with the date and
the grandchild's name and age. Then place these special
wishes into the wishing well for the future!

Off to Grandma's
House We Go!

Place a grandchild's *Special Visit* photo here.

Use Template T.

Name: _____ Age: _____

Occasion: _____

Special Memory of Visit: _____

_____

Treasures from My Closet

All dressed up with someplace to go!

Portrait Studio

Place a grandchild's
Glamour photo here.

Use Template U.

Name: _____

Age: _____

Wearing my hat, shoes, pearls, and rings,
Why, who's that dressed-up darling?

Dress-Up Fun

Name: _____

Age: _____

Let's Pretend!

Place a grandchild's
Glamour photo here.

Use Template U.

Place a grandchild's
Glamour photo here.

Use Template U.

Name: _____

Age: _____

Cherished Toys & Pets

Here are a few of their favorite things...

Place a grandchild and
Favorite Toy photo here.

Use Template V.

Name:

Age:

Favorite Toy's Name:

Place a grandchild and
Favorite Toy photo here.

Use Template V.

Name:

Age:

Favorite Toy's Name:

*"What one loves in childhood
stays in the heart forever."*

—Mary Jo Putney

Place a *grandchild and
Favorite Pet* photo here.

Use Template V.

Name: _____

Age: _____

Favorite Pet's Name: _____

Place a *grandchild and
Favorite Pet* photo here.

Use Template V.

Name: _____

Age: _____

Favorite Pet's Name: _____

Special Happenings

From concerts and recitals to school plays and sports games, record your grandchildren's special events and performances here.

Place a grandchild's
Special Event photo here.

Use Template W.

Name: _____   Age: _____

Special Event: _____

Memorable Moment: _____

_____

A Letter to
My Grandchildren

Take some time to write down all of your advice and
wisdom that you've gathered over the years so that
your grandchildren will have your thoughts to treasure for all time.
Seal your letter in this envelope to be opened at a future date.

Place a grandchild's
Special Event photo here.

Use Template W.

Name: _____

Age: _____

Special Event: _____

Memorable Moment: _____

_____

_____